THE CREATIVE CURRICULUM®
LearningGames®

36–48 Months

Joseph Sparling and Isabelle Lewis

Foreword by Diane Trister Dodge

Teaching Strategies Inc.
Washington, DC

This book of *LearningGames* is being shared with the family of

_____

Editor: Kai-leé Berke
Design: Carla Uriona
Layout/production: Tony MacFarlane and Abner Nieves

Published by:
Teaching Strategies, Inc.
P.O. Box 42243
Washington, DC 20015
www.TeachingStrategies.com

ISBN: 978-1-933021-61-4

Printed and bound in the United States of America

2012	2011	2010	2009	2008	2007
6	5	4	3	2	1

Contents

Foreword

Dear Parents,

It gives me great pleasure to introduce you to an exciting program called *The Creative Curriculum® LearningGames®*. The games are designed to build the kinds of skills that lead to successful, lifelong learning for your child. You are the key to making this happen.

On a regular basis you will be receiving a colorful handout describing simple and fun games to play with your child. They don't require any special toys or materials. You can do them as part of your everyday experiences with your child. But they can make a big difference, and they already have made a difference for thousands of children and families.

There are five different sets of *LearningGames* for children of different ages. You will receive only the games appropriate for your child. It's never too soon to start. Right from birth, your child is learning and growing. The experiences you provide during the first 5 years of life will help to build your child's brain, develop thinking skills, promote social skills, and build your child's confidence as a learner.

You are your child's first and most important teacher. Everything you do with your child, everything you say, every song you sing, and every object your give your child to play with teach important lessons. One of the wonderful results of using these games is that they help you to build a positive relationship with your child. And as your child is learning, you are as well. You will gain an understanding of child development and many practical ideas for guiding your child's learning.

Many programs using the *LearningGames* are also implementing either *The Creative Curriculum® for Infants, Toddlers & Twos* or *The Creative Curriculum® for Preschool*. As the lead author on these comprehensive curriculum materials, I am very excited to be able to offer this parent component, too. Children benefit the most when the important adults in their lives—their parents, caregivers, teachers, health care specialists, or home visitors—are working together to support their learning and growth.

I wish you great enjoyment and success,

Diane Trister Dodge
President
Teaching Strategies, Inc.

Acknowledgments

Many people helped in the preparation of *The Creative Curriculum* *LearningGames*. We would like to thank Kai-leé Berke and Heather Baker for their thoughtful writing contributions and for finding wonderful children's books that enhance each game. Thank you to Nancy Guadagno, Sharon Samber, Toni Bickart, and Rachel Tickner, our editors, for their attention to detail. We appreciate the work of Carla Uriona, who designed the new format for the activities, and Abner Nieves and Tony MacFarlane for their careful layout work. Thanks to Nancy Guadagno and Kai-leé Berke for their patience and persistence in moving the writing, editing, and production process forward.

THE CREATIVE CURRICULUM®
LearningGames®

Checklist for
The Creative Curriculum® LearningGames®:
36-48 months

I have shared the LearningGames *checked below with the family of* _____

Given to Family	LearningGames Activity Number and Title	Date Given to Family/Notes
☐	101. Soap Curls	
☐	102. A Sharing Place	
☐	103. The Duck Said...	
☐	104. Molding Shapes	
☐	105. Match and Name Pictures	
☐	106. Seeing Feelings	
☐	107. A Book About Me	
☐	108. Planting Together	
☐	109. Showing What I Know	
☐	110. A Shared Family Activity	
☐	111. Compare Two Amounts	
☐	112. Restore the Circle	
☐	113. The Knee Star	
☐	114. Prepare for Sharing	
☐	115. Stories With Three	
☐	116. What's It For?	

THE CREATIVE CURRICULUM®
LearningGames®

Given to Family	LearningGames Activity Number and Title	Date Given to Family/Notes
☐	117. Ride a Trike	
☐	118. Button and Zip	
☐	119. Two-Step Directions	
☐	120. Family Album	
☐	121. See and Show	
☐	122. Searching for Sounds	
☐	123. Painting With My Hands	
☐	124. Playing With Many Sizes	
☐	125. Move and Say	
☐	126. Showing Concern	
☐	127. Making Handprints	
☐	128. A Handy Tool	
☐	129. Painting on Paper	
☐	130. Matching Among Similar Pictures	
☐	131. That's Mine	
☐	132. I Look Great!	
☐	133. Packing My Own Picnic	
☐	134. Wear the Turn Hat	
☐	135. Plan an Event	

THE CREATIVE CURRICULUM®
LearningGames®

Given to Family	LearningGames Activity Number and Title	Date Given to Family/Notes
☐	136. Who, What, Where?	
☐	137. That Doesn't Belong	
☐	138. Ball in the Bucket	
☐	139. An Errand for Two	
☐	140. Changing Partner Roles	
☐	141. Say What Just Happened	
☐	142. Changing Things	
☐	143. Remembering Pictures	
☐	144. Copy Each Other	
☐	145. Saying All I See	
☐	146. Remember Things and Places	
☐	147. Props for Pretending	
☐	148. What Will Happen Next?	
☐	149. Letters in My Name	
☐	150. How Did You Feel When...?	

THE CREATIVE CURRICULUM®
LearningGames®

What Your Child May Be Doing
Three-Year-Olds (36–48 Months)

Social/Emotional Development

Can help make and follow a few simple rules

Imitate adult activities

Talk with other children in pairs and in groups

Are learning to take turns and share

Begin to recognize and understand the feelings of others

Enjoy simple pretend play, alone and with others

Like simple matching games

Cognitive Development

Use all of their senses to explore and investigate

Like to gather information about the world

Are interested in cause and effect (what makes things happen)

Ask why questions

Sort and categorize materials

Physical Development

Walk, run, and turn with coordination

Walk along a line, using arms for balance

Climb stairs using alternate feet

Jump with two feet

Hop and balance on one foot

Push and pedal tricycles

Throw, catch, and kick large balls

Use utensils to eat and serve themselves

Dress themselves and use large fasteners

Coordinate eye and hand movements (for example, pour water into a funnel, create a tall block structure)

Turn pages one at a time

Use tools to draw simple shapes and objects

Language and Literacy Development

Use language to gain information, understand concepts, express feelings, and make requests

Participate in conversations with adults

Tell simple stories as they look at pictures and books

Enjoy a wide variety of books

Learn print concepts, such as reading a book from front to back and reading a page from top to bottom

Use speech that is easy to understand; use three-to-five word sentences

Soap Curls

The shampoo makes your hair stand up!

When bathing your child, lather his hair thickly with shampoo so that you can shape his hair in several ways.

Your child will be entertained at bath time and will have a chance to see himself in a new way.

Why this is important

Your child can get more out of shampoo than clean hair. He can enjoy seeing his image change in the mirror. This game can help make your child comfortable and familiar with his image even as things change.

What you do

- Use shampoo to create a thick lather in your child's hair.

- Hold a small hand mirror for him to see his new look.

- Shape the lather and let your child see himself in several new hair styles. Pull his hair up into a tall peak or form many small spikes on his head.

- Watch his response, and take your cue from him. If he laughs, say, *What funny, tall hair you have!*

- Add more hair shapes to the game, or try a soap beard and sideburns.

Ready to move on?

Challenge his hand-eye coordination by offering him a second mirror to view the back of his head. Demonstrate how to hold two mirrors in order to view the back. Offer to hold one mirror if he cannot hold both successfully.

Let's read together!

The Hair Book
by Todd Parr

A Sharing Place

Yes, there you are with Grandma in the park. That was a fun day.

Grandma!

Create a space in your home where your family can share objects with each other.

Your child will enjoy sharing, talking, and hearing what other family members say.

THE CREATIVE CURRICULUM® **LearningGames**®

Copyright 2007 Joseph Sparling

Why this is important

Your child may enjoy sharing but may also need help doing it. You can encourage and expand this behavior by providing a family sharing place. Together you will talk about the shared items. Words will become the principal way of sharing as your child grows, and he will enjoy the stories that accompany each object. He will learn that although he cannot take home all objects and experiences, he can share them through his words and drawings, and later with his letters and photographs.

What you do

- Find a space in your home to dedicate to sharing. The space should include a flat surface and an upright surface for hanging items. You can use a box or low shelf with a cork board or cloth hanging behind. Make sure the flat space is within your child's reach. **If you hang items on a cork board, make sure thumb tacks or push pins are kept out of your child's reach.**

- Draw your child's attention to an object on display: *Look, Alex, here's a letter. It's from Grandma. She sent us a new picture.*

- Give him time to handle the object and then later share it with other family members. He may ask questions about the item to help him remember it.

- Encourage your child to share an object with you, and then thank him for his contribution to the sharing space.

Another idea

Remind your child about the sharing place when walking outside or playing in the park. Help him find interesting objects throughout his day that he can place in the sharing space. You can also encourage him to display his artwork for everyone to enjoy.

Let's read together!

David's Drawings
by Cathryn Falwell

The Duck Said...

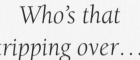

Who's that tripping over...

...my bridge!

Read a familiar book to your child and pause in the middle of a repeated line.

Your child will practice using words by filling in the blanks of the familiar story.

Why this is important

When you read stories to children they hear many new words used in different ways. Your child will increase her understanding, memory, and use of words as she listens to a story. She may also begin to notice printed words on a page. Her experiences of listening and helping to tell a story will help her learn to love reading. Completing, or filling in, a familiar sentence is an easy way for her to practice her memory skills and use her growing vocabulary.

What you do

- Choose a familiar story, such as *The Little Red Hen*, which has repeated words and sounds.

- Invite your child to say the repetitive lines in the story as you read. For example, when the Hen asks who will plant the wheat, you can read, *The Duck said…* Then let her fill in the words, *Not I!*

- Point to the words as she says them. Later, encourage her to point to the words.

- Challenge her by leaving out a word that shows the sequence of the story. For example, read *Who will help me…this wheat?* She will need to choose from several words (*plant, water, cut,* or *eat*) by remembering what has already happened and what comes next.

Another idea

You can keep your child interested in this activity by choosing funny stories with repeated noises and sounds. Stories about animals, machines that act like people, or families and familiar situations provide fun opportunities for your child to contribute to telling the story.

Let's read together!

The Little Red Hen
by Byron Barton

Molding Shapes

This is my sun!

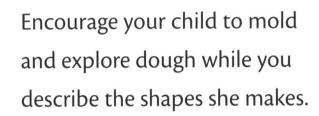

Encourage your child to mold and explore dough while you describe the shapes she makes.

Your child will begin to connect the shapes she feels with her hands with the shape words she hears you say.

Why this is important

Molding dough gives your child the experience of learning how three-dimensional shapes are formed. The experiences children gain directly through using their hands and fingers leave a special and lasting understanding of the physical world. Easy art exploration can give your child confidence for later creative expressions.

What you do

● Give your child opportunities to press and mold soft materials, such as playdough. Help your child dampen a clay or dirt area outside in order to make mud. Explain in advance that this is a messy activity! Let her explore freely without direction.

● Describe what she is doing as she plays. *You've made something flat and round. What a long coil! You pushed your thumb all the way through the middle.*

● Try making playdough using the following recipe:

2 cups flour	1 cup water
1 cup salt	2 tablespooons cooking oil
2 tablespooons cream of tartar	1 tablespoon food coloring

Mix all ingredients together in a saucepan. Cook over low–medium heat, stirring constantly until it forms a ball. Put the ball on a board and knead for 2–3 minutes. Store the dough in an airtight container between play sessions.

Another idea

Renew your child's interest in the game and extend your child's creativity by offering tools to press and shape the dough: popsicle sticks, sea shells, rocks, or pipe cleaners. **Make sure that these items do not go into your child's mouth. Put away things small enough to swallow when you cannot supervise their use, especially if you use this game with children under age 3.**

Let's read together!

Sun Bread
by Elisa Kleven

Match and Name Pictures

Yes! You found two that are the same. What are those called?

Mix up pairs of identical pictures and ask your child to find matches and name them.

Your child will learn to recognize which pictures are the same and may say the name of each one.

Why this is important

Your child will learn to recognize similarities between pictures as he learns the name of each pictured object. Although your child may not clearly name the pictures at first, he will learn to recognize and match them as you say the names. By first hearing and then repeating the name, he may begin to link pictures to various sounds, ideas, and vocabulary.

What you do

- Gather two identical copies of 10 or more pictures. Attach the pictures to cards to make them sturdy.

- Place four cards (two of them identical) face up in front of your child. Invite him to find the two that are the same. He may point to or pick up the cards.

- Respond to his choice by saying: *Yes, these two are alike. These are called tomatoes.* You do not need to label the other pictures.

- Shuffle the cards back into the original stack and play again.

- Encourage your child to name the pictures after becoming familiar with the game. *What are these called?*

- Tell him the word for the picture if he needs help: *You know what it looks like to me? It looks like a bulldozer. Can you say* bulldozer?

- Encourage him to stack each matching pair so that he builds a pile of matching cards.

Another idea

As he gets comfortable with the game, add more pairs to each round. Try three or four pairs of cards, and space them so that he must look thoroughly to find each matching set. Encourage him to name all the pictures as he plays.

Let's read together!

The Very Hungry Caterpillar
by Eric Carle

Seeing Feelings

Talk with your child about what people around him are feeling.

Naming the emotions your child sees helps him begin to recognize and understand them.

Do you think Tawanda is feeling a little left out and sad?

THE
CREATIVE CURRICULUM®
LearningGames®
Copyright 2007 Joseph Sparling

Why this is important

Children notice people around them expressing feelings, but they do not have the experience to fully understand what they see. By pointing out and naming emotions when they occur in peers, you help your child recognize what others are feeling. He will have more success interacting with others when he begins to pay attention to the feelings of the people around him. Recognizing another person's emotion is one step in the difficult task of understanding another person's point of view.

What you do

- Point out the feelings of siblings or neighborhood children. Draw your child's attention to another child's strong emotional expression: *I think Matt looks very happy now.*

- Talk more about what has made the other child feel that way. *Holding that balloon really put a smile on Matt's face.*

- Move on to a new topic if your child shows no interest. From time to time, continue to point out feelings and to name them.

- Offer encouragement when your child notices someone's feelings on his own. *You're paying attention to other people's feelings. You noticed Sara was sad.*

- Comment on feelings that may frighten your child: *Chris is so angry right now. I'm glad his Nana is there to help him. I think he will feel better soon.*

- Encourage your child to help a child who feels sad: *Harry looks sad—with tears in his eyes. I wonder if it's because he dropped his cupcake? I think I'll see if he needs some help. Would you like to come with me?*

Another idea

Encourage your child to name the emotions he sees, beginning with happy, angry, and sad. The names of other emotions, such as suspicious, frustrated, and excited, may take longer for your child to recognize and say.

Let's read together!

Today I Feel Silly
by Jamie Lee Curtis

A Book About Me

Your book tells a lot about you.

Encourage your child to save items that are important to him, and help him put them in a book.

Your child can use the book to share important aspects of his life with friends and family.

Why this is important

Your child knows many different facts about himself. You can help him bring those facts together in a book. Collecting personal items in a book gives your child a reason to feel proud. This book also provides a resource that your child can review again at any time and may be a source of identity and security for your child.

What you do

- Help your child collect items that represent his favorite things. For example, *You like peaches so much. Let's save the label from this basket of peaches.*

- Encourage him to set aside special mementos. For example, these could include a leaf from his favorite climbing tree, one of his drawings, or a postcard he receives.

- Fasten together several sheets of construction paper to make a book.

- Add a title to the cover, such as *A Book About Jon*, or ask your child what he would like to call his book.

- Invite him to decorate the cover of the book. Let your child attach the mementos to each page using glue or tape.

- Talk about each page as he assembles it: *This page reminds me that your Grandma loves you and writes to you. And this shows how much you like to draw with your crayons.*

- Make sure to include empty pages in the book so that he can add more items later.

Another idea

Encourage your child to share his album with friends and family. Write a few simple words next to a picture such as *My pet* or *I found*. He may not use many words to describe each page, but he will enjoy sharing his life with others. Invite family members to ask him questions about his book.

Let's read together!

I Like Me!
by Nancy Carlson

Planting Together

Good, you're getting the dirt right in there.

Create a window garden with your child and talk to him about how you worked together to make the window garden grow.

Your child will gain experience in cooperating and taking responsibility.

Here are the things we need for our garden.

THE CREATIVE CURRICULUM® LearningGames®

Why this is important

Completing one part of a group task is an early form of cooperation. By participating in a family project, your child will learn to be a partner in getting the job done. Those roles will carry over into school and, later, into his adult life.

What you do

- Choose a sunny windowsill to grow a family garden together. If possible, you may create your garden outside.

- Make a list of needed items with your child and other members of the family, and together collect a few things such as seeds, potting soil, water, paper or plastic cups, etc.

- Begin by putting potting soil in each cup. Give your child as many opportunities to help as possible.

- Ask him to put the seeds in the cups. Choose seeds that sprout and grow quickly, such as green peas or any kind of bean. Demonstrate how to push the seed down into the soil.

- Explain to your child that the plant needs time to grow. Talk about how each plant needs soil, light, and water.

- Place a watering schedule near the window. Each person can take turns watering. Let your child check off his name on the schedule after his turn. *You watered the plants when it was your turn. When we all remember our turns, the plants get what they need to grow.*

- Let your child watch and imitate your care for the plants.

Another idea

Talk about how each plant is growing taller. Encourage your child to draw pictures of the plants to document the growth. Create more jobs involving the plants such as making stick supports for the plants.

Let's read together!

Red Leaf, Yellow Leaf
by Lois Ehlert

Showing What I Know

Put your finger on something that's purple.

Name or describe a picture you see in a magazine or book and invite your child to point to it on the page.

Your child will have an opportunity to practice hearing and understanding many words.

THE
CREATIVE CURRICULUM®
LearningGames®
Copyright 2007 Joseph Sparling

Why this is important

Naming or describing the pictures you see and then inviting your child to point to them on the page allows him to practice hearing and understanding words. Reading books with him helps him practice using his ability to understand words. This game can help you and your child become aware of the different kinds of things he knows.

What you do

- Invite your child to sit with you and look at a book. Choose a children's book or a family magazine, and pause on pages that interest both of you.

- Ask questions that will let your child demonstrate his knowledge, especially knowledge that goes beyond his spoken vocabulary. A few examples of questions are:

    Can you find something that goes fast?

    Which plate has two cookies on it?

    Can you point to the spaghetti?

    Which picture has an open window in it?

- Observe your child thinking about the question and pointing to the answer.

- Follow your child's lead and adjust the difficulty of the game by choosing a book with many pictures on the page, or continue to use a book with only a few pictures.

Another idea

Play the game many times by varying the books or magazines and the questions. When you come to a picture that you know your child is able to say, let him name it and ask you to point. If your child recognizes any letters, invite him to point to and name them as well.

Let's read together!

Bark George
by Jules Feiffer

A Shared Family Activity

Those birds will love that peanut butter.

You're scooping out those seeds carefully.

Give your child the opportunity to feel like an important member of the family by involving him in shared activities.

Your child will learn group values and cooperation when participating in a shared activity.

THE CREATIVE CURRICULUM®
LearningGames®

Why this is important

You can help your child feel included in activities or hobbies that have value in your family's culture. He will value activities that make him feel good and that are important to your family. Having a specific job in a shared, family-valued task, such as filling the scoop with birdseed, lets your child feel needed, and he will feel satisfaction when he watches the birds eat the seeds that he helped to prepare. Participating in a shared task builds his understanding of why your family values the activity.

What you do

- Include your child in plans and events that convey your family's values. For example, when you feed birds, let him use his hands to mix the seeds in a large container. (Of course, choose whatever family activity is important to your own family.)

- Invite him to make something that is important to your family. For example, invite him to create a birdfeeder by covering a pinecone with peanut butter and then rolling it in birdseed.

- Talk to him about what he is doing. For example, describe the big and little seeds for big and little birds.

- Take time after he completes his task to sit together and share your thoughts about the event. *I know the birds are going to be happy to get these seeds.*

Another idea

Invite your child to draw a picture about the event. Let him tell you about what happened and what he did. You can record his words on his picture so you can re-read it with him later.

Let's read together!

The Great Trash Bash
by Loreen Leedy

Compare Two Amounts

Yes, you showed me the one that has less dough.

Give your child something to play with, such as playdough or water, that can be divided into two parts.

You can help your child notice amounts and talk about them using the words *more* and *less*.

Why this is important

Recognizing the difference between two amounts is the basis for many math concepts. Your child will enjoy grouping, dividing, and pouring to create amounts she can label with *more* and *less*. Later, she will use her skills to arrange items in a series.

What you do

- Provide playdough for your child.

- Notice when she divides her playdough: *You made this into two different parts. Look, this ball has more playdough and this ball has less.*

- Move the balls around on the table and say, *Point to the one that has more dough. Point to the one that has less.*

- Continue the game by pressing the dough back together and then making a new ball from part of the dough.

- Show her the ball you made and suggest that she make a smaller ball, one with less dough. Describe the balls using the words *more* and *less*.

- Encourage her to use the words by asking, *How much dough does this one have? How much does the other one have?* Help her with the words as needed.

Another idea

Play the game again using two identical cups with water. Your child will learn a new form of more and less by looking at the level of the water in the cups. Then try other materials and containers, such as sand in buckets, air in balloons, or yogurt in bowls.

Let's read together!

Little Rabbits' First Number Book
by Alan Baker

Restore the Circle

Cut a large paper circle into two pieces and let your child fit the two pieces together to form the circle again.

Your child will see that things can be divided and restored.

You're making it into a circle.

THE
CREATIVE CURRICULUM®
Learning Games®

Why this is important

Being able to visualize the whole from its parts is necessary for many tasks your child will want to do. She will learn to recognize that actions such as dividing a circle can be reversed. Letters and numbers are typically made from parts such as lines and circles, so this game helps her get ready to recognize number and letter symbols.

What you do

- Cut out a few large paper circles. Invite your child to play a new game with you.

- Show her one of the circles and talk about what makes it a circle: *This is a circle. Look at its round shape.*

- Hold the circle and let her trace her finger around the edge. Place the circle on the table and, with her hand on top of your hand, trace the entire edge of the circle.

- Think of words such as *plate*, *pie*, and *circle* to describe the shape.

- Use scissors to cut the paper in half. Show her each curved piece.

- Ask her to put the circle back together.

- Trace the finished circle again and tell her, *You made it a circle again!*

- Try cutting the circle into several pieces to make the game a little harder. Make sure you keep the game short and stop when she loses interest.

Ready to move on?

Other shapes, such as triangles and squares, are harder to restore. Move on to these shapes when your child is immediately successful with the circle. Adjust the difficulty of the game by changing the number of pieces you create when cutting the shape.

Let's read together!

I Spy Shapes In Art
by Lucy Micklethwait

The Knee Star

Here's a star for your knee.

Put a star sticker or some other marker on a part of your child's body and talk about that part throughout the day.

Your child will learn to locate body parts and recognize their names.

THE
CREATIVE CURRICULUM®
LearningGames®

Copyright 2007 Joseph Sparling

Why this is important

Knowing the words for body parts helps your child understand when other people talk about them. You can give your child markers that help locate body parts and connect them with their names. Knowing words that refer to his own body helps him build a better understanding of himself.

What you do

- Begin by playing a quick review game to find out which body parts your child already knows. Say, *Touch your neck. Touch your elbow. Touch your ankle.*

- Choose a body part your child is not aware of. Then, make it clear where that body part is by marking it. For example, if you choose *knee*, make it clear where his knee is by putting a star sticker on it.

- Remind him during the day about where to find his knee: *I see that you're bending your knees. Your knees are under the table when you sit in that chair.*

- Think about body parts that are not used every day such as shin, knuckle, and sole. Find an interesting way to mark each one you teach.

- Invite your child to go back and rename each part as he adds to his list of words.

Another idea

Help your child recognize body parts on others by inviting him to find your shin, ankle, etc. He can also find the parts on a doll as he finds them on his own body.

Let's read together!

Toes, Ears, & Nose!
by Karen Katz

Prepare for Sharing

You girls are using that wagon together.

Create an opportunity for sharing by offering toys such as puppets and wagons to your child and a friend.

You will encourage sharing by giving the children toys that work best when shared and by encouraging their efforts to play together.

Two people can get a lot of sand in the bucket.

Why this is important

By arranging a play space that makes sharing and cooperation more likely, you encourage your child to practice sharing materials and equipment with other children. Explaining to the children when they should take turns, work together, or trade helps your child learn to value sharing. This game helps your child get ready for more complex tasks that are accomplished through a group effort.

What you do

- Look for opportunities to create sharing moments between your child and others.

- Arrange a special play corner indoors where children can play together. Start with two children and invite more friends as your child feels comfortable sharing.

- Offer a few duplicate toys so that not all toys need to be shared. Include puppets or blocks that encourage interaction between children.

- Outside, try inviting the children to use a wagon. One child can pull while another rides.

- Notice any cooperation and respond positively: *Edwina, you hopped right out of the wagon and gave Joni a turn before she even said she was tired of pulling. You girls are sharing the wagon like such good friends.*

Another idea

Use an egg timer or portable oven timer with a bell if the children need help knowing when to trade toys. Explain the timer to the children. *Everyone gets a turn to play with the truck. Let's set the timer. When the bell rings, it's time to trade.*

Let's read together!

Yo! Yes!
by Chris Raschka

Stories With Three

Can you count the chairs?

When reading books that illustrate the concept of *three*, stop and let your child count items that come in threes.

Your child will gain a fuller understanding of the number *three* by hearing it in stories and by counting.

One for daddy bear…

THE
CREATIVE CURRICULUM®
LearningGames®

Why this is important

Now that your child is 3 years old, he may show interest in objects that come in threes. You can strengthen his concept of *three* by telling traditional stories that are built around the number three.

What you do

- Bring the number *three* to your child's attention by telling or reading stories with threes such as *Three Perfect Peaches, The Three Bears, The Three Little Pigs,* and *The Three Billy Goats Gruff.*

- Emphasize the number *three* in the title: *Let's read the story* The Three Bears. *Look, here are their pictures: 1, 2, 3. Three bears.*

- Count items in the story that are grouped in threes such as the bowls, chairs, or beds.

- Have your child use objects such as blocks, clothespins, or crackers as counters. Help your child practice handling groups of three: *Count out some crackers to show how many bears there were in the story. Yes! Let's put that group over here. Now can you count out more crackers to show how many bowls there were?*

- Encourage your child to do most of the counting and talking as you move through the story or count objects. Play this game with different books and objects to help your child learn that *three* is a word and a concept used to describe three items.

Another idea

Look for books with three wishes, three tasks, three fairies, etc. You can go to your local library and ask for help in finding stories with a theme of *three.*

Let's read together!

The Three Bears
by Byron Barton

What's It For?

Is that something to build with?

No!

As you look at various objects and pictures with your child, ask a question about the purpose of the item.

Your child will practice grouping objects by thinking about what they are used for.

Which of these things can we build with?

THE CREATIVE CURRICULUM®
LearningGames®

Why this is important

Classifying items into groups is a basic way to organize our knowledge. Your child will have the chance to practice sorting as she hears the names of categories that explain the uses and functions of objects. By guiding your child to focus on items one at a time, you are showing her how to deal with big tasks slowly and systematically.

What you do

- Gather several objects or pictures of objects. Spread the objects out in front of your child and invite her to play.

- Start by saying, *Some of these are things we can wear. Let's find out which ones.*

- Let your child examine each object as you talk about it.

- Keep your questions age-appropriate. Use *Yes/No* questions if your child is unable to say more about an item. Confirm her answers to let her know that you understand her: *You're right, I can't imagine anyone wearing a crayon! Let's put that over here in a pile of things you can't wear.*

- Challenge your child to use each object, even if her first guess at classifying is incorrect. *Can you wear that book on your head? No, I guess it goes in the other pile, right?*

- Continue the game until all the objects are classified.

- Try categories such as *things we ride, things we use to eat, things we read*, etc.

Another idea

You can make the game more active by placing the piles around the room. Your child will need to pick up each object, examine it, and then carry it to the appropriate pile.

Let's read together!

Around the House
by Victoria Huseby

Ride a Trike

Describe your child's experience as she rides a tricycle.

You can provide a safe environment and teach her new words as your child learns this fun motor skill.

Good steering! You're riding right down this path.

THE CREATIVE CURRICULUM®
LearningGames®

Why this is important

Riding a tricycle can provide your child with a new way of getting around. She must learn to move the trike and steer at the same time. She must make decisions about slowing down and stopping while riding something that moves faster than she can walk. Use this opportunity to teach her words that describe space and action. Helping her feel safe on a tricycle builds her confidence as she gains control of the trike.

What you do

- Show your child the tricycle, and then leave it in her play space for her to explore when she feels ready. **Make sure your child always wears a helmet when riding. Even when she practices simply sitting on the bike, she can get used to the feeling of wearing a helmet.**

- Notice how she discovers the ways the trike moves. She may sit on it, turn it upside down and spin the wheels, or turn the handlebars back and forth.

- Use words to help her talk about her actions. For direction, she can learn *turn*, *ahead*, *path*, and *guide*. For movement, teach her *slow*, *fast*, *stop*, and *go*. And for the tricycle she can learn *pedal*, *handlebars*, *wheels*, and *seat*.

- Offer ideas about what she can expect when riding: *When you're ready to make that turn, you will need to slow down. Do you think the path between the posts is wide enough to go through?*

- Give her your full attention and occasional direction as she builds her skills. Although it may seem fun to invite her friends to ride along, it is important for her to ride alone while she learns to control the tricycle.

Another idea

Make a few road signs, such as *stop* and *go*, that will help her learn the rules of riding.

Let's read together!

Do Princesses Scrape Their Knees?
by Carmela LaVigna Coyle

Button and Zip

Lead your child through the steps of buttoning and unbuttoning and zipping and unzipping.

Your child will become more confident with her personal care skills of dressing and undressing.

> *You're moving that zipper up, up, up.*

THE
CREATIVE CURRICULUM®
LearningGames®
Copyright 2007 Joseph Sparling

Why this is important

Guiding your child in learning to button and zip helps her learn the skills needed for independent dressing. Children who are struggling to be independent often are unwilling to accept the help they need. By learning the more difficult steps like buttoning and zipping, she will be able to take care of her own dressing at home or school.

What you do

- Give your child a smock or sweater with large buttons and buttonholes. Explain and demonstrate how to put the button through the buttonhole.

- Show her how to push the button halfway through the hole. Then, hold that part of the button as she pulls the cloth over the other half.

- Keep a few garments handy that have easy-to-fasten buttons. Let her practice during a long car ride or while waiting at the doctor's office. Encourage her to button her own clothes when she is ready.

- Teach her how to zip a zipper by letting her zip up your coat for you. Explain how to hold the bottom of the coat as she pulls up on the zipper.

- Resist the urge to finish the job for her. She needs lots of practice to master this skill!

Another idea

Invite your child to practice buttoning and zipping in front of a mirror. Encourage her to show a friend or relative what she is learning.

Let's read together!

Zippers, Buttons, and Bows
by Moira Butterfield

Two-Step Directions

> *Take the papers out of the box, and then you can use it as a picnic table.*

Offer your child directions that ask for two or more actions.

Two-step directions give your child practice in understanding and completing all the parts of a task.

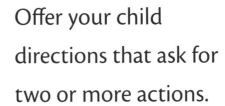

THE
CREATIVE CURRICULUM®
LearningGames®
Copyright 2007 Joseph Sparling

Why this is important

Your child can learn to follow clear, multi-step directions when you give her opportunities to practice. Following directions is very important in school, and people follow verbal and written directions throughout their lives. Participation in most shared activities involves giving or following directions.

What you do

- Use this game frequently and over a long period of time (a year or more) to give your child an opportunity to practice following directions in many situations.

- Make the game relaxed and use a friendly tone of voice so that your child feels encouraged to listen to you. Begin with directions that ask for two actions: *Please find your boots and put them in the closet.*

- Create directions to lead her to a surprise: *Look in the grocery bag, and then take what you find to the table for our snack.*

- Keep your directions simple with two actions at first. As she confidently completes the tasks, add more directions until there are three or four steps.

- Remember to thank her for finishing the task, if appropriate. *Thanks! You did exactly what I asked.* Offer encouragement for a job well done. *You looked in the bag and put our surprise snack on the table! Now we can eat our yummy graham crackers.*

Another idea

Use school words, such as *crayons, scissors, books, tables,* and *chairs,* to help your child prepare for hearing and following directions in the classroom. A few examples of directions she may hear in school are: *Put some newspaper down before you begin to paint. When you get up, push your chair in, please. Take a book from the shelf and then go and sit where we can read a story.*

Let's read together!

Pete's A Pizza
by William Steig

Family Album

What does Daddy like to eat?

Help your child make an album of photos and facts about his family.

The process will help your child organize and express his knowledge of his family.

Tell me about our family.

THE
CREATIVE CURRICULUM®
LearningGames®
Copyright 2007 Joseph Sparling

Why this is important

A simple album can remind young children of their substantial family knowledge and family relationships. Creating an album will help your child think about the members of his family and what they do. An album also may increase your child's enjoyment of books, pictures, and print.

What you do

- Take a week or more to help your child create an album that tells something about his family.

- Create a page for each family member by gluing or taping a photo of that person to a sheet of paper.

- Help your child choose a family member each day to think about: *What is Mommy's favorite food? Favorite color? An activity she likes?*

- Encourage your child to ask the family member if he does not already know the answers to your questions.

- Help him search through magazines to find pictures that represent the answer to each question. Give him glue or tape to attach the pictures to the photo page. Or, offer him some crayons or markers to see if he would like to draw the pictures.

- Build the story of his family, one member at a time, until all pages are completed.

- Ask your child to decorate a page to use as the cover, and then fasten the pages together to make a book.

- Take time to review the book together, and invite your child to share the book with others.

Another idea

Invite your child to share his family album with a visitor. You may enjoy hearing how your child describes his family and the details he remembers.

Let's read together!

All Families Are Special
by Norma Simon

See and Show

The third thing you do is blow on the paint.

Show your child how to use a straw to make a painting and encourage him to explain the process to someone else.

Great! Would you like to show Melissa how to do this?

This experience allows your child to practice sharing useful information with others.

Why this is important

When you demonstrate a process for your child to share with others, he will need to pay close attention so that he can show it to someone else. When he uses words to explain the steps in a process, he is practicing narration, one of the skills in early literacy.

What you do

- Invite your child to watch you make a straw painting. As you demonstrate, let him know that later he will have the important job of teaching someone.

- Organize your instruction into three main parts so they will be easy to remember.

- Explain that first he must put a piece of painting paper down on a few sheets of newspaper. Second, place a few drops of paint on the paper. The third step is to blow gently through the straw to scatter the paint around. This will make interesting designs on the paper.

- Let him decide which friend or family member he would like to teach. Encourage him to use both words and actions as he teaches.

- Review briefly the steps in the process: *Now, what is the first thing you will show?* Continue to talk through the remaining steps.

- Position yourself near the new teacher and student, but do not intervene unless needed.

- Respond positively to both your child and the one he is teaching. *Michael, you explained the three steps so clearly! Jesse, you blew green and purple paint around your paper!*

Another idea

A few other easy-to-teach projects are making a peanut butter sandwich, planting seeds in a pot, and rolling a ball of dough.

Let's read together!

I'll Teach My Dog a Lot of Words
by Michael Frith

Searching for Sounds

What kind of sound could this make?

Find various objects around the house and describe the sound your child can make with each object.

Your child becomes more familiar with his environment when he has the chance to hear and classify sounds.

Why this is important

A surprising variety of sounds can be made around the house. Exposure to these sounds helps your child recognize, label, and describe them. Knowing and classifying everyday sounds are part of your child's growing awareness of the world. Since sounds occur and then are gone, they demand a different kind of thinking and memory than do objects that will remain in view.

What you do

- Walk around the room with your child, and stop near various objects as you wonder aloud, *What kind of sound could this make?* Encourage your child to experiment with the object to create sound.

- Describe any sound your child makes, such as with a pan and spoon: *Listen to the loud* clang, clang, clang!

- Show him how various objects can make different sounds. For example, drop a small, plastic toy into the sink: *I hear a soft splash.*

- Review the sounds with your child at the end of the game: *Let's think about the sounds that we just made and decide which ones were loud and which ones were soft. First, we heard the sound the pan made. Was it loud or soft?*

Another idea

Search for sounds outdoors, listening for sounds you do not make, such as sounds from crickets, cars, or airplanes.

Let's read together!

The Listening Walk
by Paul Showers

Painting With My Hands

You're making a new color: orange.

Invite your child to explore with finger paints as you describe the process and the marks she makes.

Your child may begin to notice the relationship between her hand movements and the marks made on the page.

THE CREATIVE CURRICULUM®
LearningGames®

Why this is important

Finger painting is a fun, sensory art experience. Through experimenting with finger paints, your child will begin to notice the relationship between her movements and the marks she creates. Allowing your child to freely explore the paints on a large, flat surface gives her the chance to develop her creative expression.

What you do

- Put a smock on your child to protect clothing.

- Use finger paint directly on a table with a wipe-clean surface, or use a cookie sheet or cover your table with a plastic shower curtain to protect your table top. Dampen the surface with a sponge and then put a spoonful of paint in front of your child.

- Stand back and enjoy watching your child freely move the paint around on the table. She may work more easily while standing to allow for larger arm movement.

- Observe and comment on what you see your child making: *You moved your arm in a big circle and now there is a circle in the red paint.*

- Give your child one color at a time as she learns how the paint works on the table.

- Later add another color to the activity. Start with a light color, such as yellow, and add a small amount of red or blue. Your child will enjoy watching the colors change.

Another idea

Save a copy of the finished artwork by pressing a sheet of newsprint on the table and then carefully peeling the paper away. This makes a print of your child's table painting on the paper. Lay it flat until the paint is dry.

Let's read together!

My Hands
by Aliki

Playing With Many Sizes

Big, big, little, little

Offer your child objects that are graduated in size, such as a canister set or measuring cups, and respond to the way she arranges them.

Your child will begin to learn about the math skill of sequencing items by size.

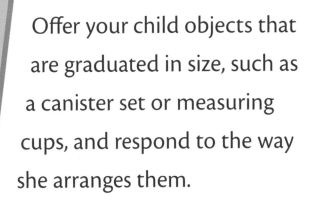

THE
CREATIVE CURRICULUM®
LearningGames®

Why this is important

Playing with objects of graduated size encourages your child to create arrangements and sequences based on size or amount. This skill is needed for determining the differences among a series of sizes, such as in clothing, food portions, and tools. It will help your child make choices when she is able to understand where any one item fits in a series.

What you do

- Find safe household objects for your child to play with that are graduated in size, such as measuring spoons, canisters, nesting toys, or graduated wrenches. You also can create groups of shoes or jar lids in varying sizes.

- Show your child one set of objects and invite her to play: *Here are a set of six measuring spoons. Let's see what you can do with them.* (If you use measuring spoons or cups, make sure they are separate and not joined on a ring.)

- Wait for your child to notice the different sizes and begin to compare the items. Give her plenty of time to play without assistance.

- When you notice your child comparing sizes, talk about size relationships: *You put them all in a row. Let's see, this is the smallest one at this end. What did you put at the other end?*

- Invite your child to record her accomplishment by placing the row of items on a piece of paper and tracing around each one.

Let's read together!

Swimmy
by Leo Lionni

Ready to move on?

Challenge your child to notice a different type of size relationship by filling a few identical plastic cups with varying levels of water. When she arranges them correctly, add more water to (or pour some water out of) one or two glasses so that she can find a new order.

Move and Say

You're going around the red tub.

Around.

Invite your child to maneuver around a small obstacle course while you describe his body motions.

Your child will gain experience using position words to talk about what he is doing.

Why this is important

The best way for your child to learn action words is to hear them and say them just at the moment he is engaged in doing them. Performing the actions increases his understanding of positions in space. Knowing the words for spatial relationships increases his understanding of situations and instructions. For example, *Go around the puddle to the car* is quite different from *Go to the car.*

What you do

- Use a garden hose or rope to mark an interesting path for your child to follow.

- Describe his movements as he moves along the path: *through the box tunnel, under the bench, over the block.*

- Invite him to say the words first with you and then encourage him to describe his position by himself. *Where will you go next?*

- Add new challenges to the path to increase his physical skills. Try incorporating a small plastic lid that he can stand on with one foot or a one-inch wide tape for walking on a line.

- Describe more subtle movements such as *walk next to the box, jump away from the paper, go around the puddle,* or *tiptoe along the line.*

- Periodically, reposition the obstacles to provide new actions and help him learn new positions.

- Walk him through the path the first time you use the new position words.

Ready to move on?

Play a game with one rule: Your child must say the word that describes his action as he does it.

Let's read together!

Copy Me Copycub
by Richard Edwards

Showing Concern

You're giving your doll a bandage to help her feel better.

Oh, that's just what your doll needs: a hug.

Help your child use a doll to learn how to respond to strong emotions.

Responding to a doll's pretend emotions gives your child a chance to practice sympathy and learn various ways of comforting someone.

THE
CREATIVE CURRICULUM®
LearningGames®

Why this is important

Your child can begin to practice feelings of concern or sympathy by responding to the imaginary needs of a doll. You can role-play real problem situations in order to guide your child and teach her how to express concern. Showing personal concern is part of learning to help and care for others.

What you do

- Invite your child to play with a doll after witnessing another child display strong emotion.

- Start by saying: *This doll fell down and skinned his knee, just like Jimmy did a few minutes ago. What can we do for this doll?*

- Give your child time to make suggestions such as a bandage or wet cloth.

- Hold the doll to show your child another way to provide comfort. When she imitates the action, respond with positive feedback: *Oh, I see that you're going to comfort him. The doll needs some love as much as he needs the bandage.*

- Include various scenarios such as a sad doll that needs cheering up or an angry doll that your child could help to calm.

Ready to move on?

After your child has had a number of opportunities to respond to a doll's emotions, begin to encourage her to respond helpfully to the feelings of her playmates. *Jimmy looks a little sad right now. Do you think you might be able to cheer him up?* Do not expect every effort to be successful, but your child will feel good when she makes another child feel better.

Let's read together!

Unknown
by Colin Thompson

Making Handprints

Let's count the fingers.

You made a handprint!

Show your child how to make a picture of her hand using finger paints.

Making a print of her own hand gives your child a special way to express her individuality.

Why this is important

Seeing a print of her own hand can help your child become more aware of herself as a unique person. Your child may enjoy tracking her growth by comparing her current handprint to one she made as a baby.

What you do

- Offer your child a blank sheet of paper at the end of a finger-painting session.

- Ask her to press her hand lightly into the paint, then firmly onto the paper.

- Observe her reaction to the design. Does she recognize the picture of her hand? Does she try it again? Does she want to repeat with the other hand? Does she look to you to share what she just did?

- Explain that the handprints are a kind of picture of herself: *You made a picture of your hand! Thank you for sharing your special art with me. It looks like you are going to make a blue handprint with your other hand now.*

- Encourage your child to look at her handprint next to yours or those of other family members. She can count fingers on her hand and on the other prints to discover they have the same number. You can point out that each handprint is slightly different, which makes each person special.

- Invite her to have fun making handprints on various washable surfaces both indoors and outdoors. She can put handprints on the refrigerator, bathroom mirror, or counter top.

Another idea

Your child can use her handprint as her personal signature in letters to relatives. Her handprints made on paper can be saved and displayed or sent to loved ones who want to see how she is growing.

Let's read together!

These Hands
by Hope Lynne Price

A Handy Tool

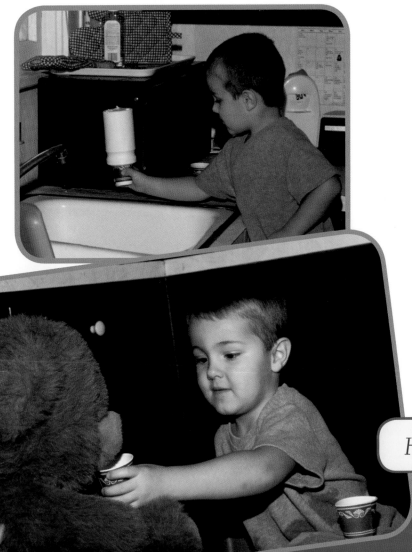

Put some paper cups or other useful things in a handy place that your child can reach and invite him to use these items for tools in various ways.

You can encourage your child's independence by making helpful objects available to him.

Have a drink.

CREATIVE CURRICULUM®
LearningGames®

Why this is important

As we grow, our need for tools increases. Early and varied opportunities to use tools help your child think creatively about objects and problem solving. Keeping useful household objects readily available for your child encourages independence.

What you do

- Encourage your child to use everyday objects, such as paper cups, as tools that help him complete tasks independently.

- Make the items easily available to him so that he can think of various ways to use them. For example, he can use a paper cup as a bowl for his dolls, a scoop in the sandbox, a watering can for his potted plant, or a temporary home for a snail he finds.

- Offer positive feedback for his ideas: *Using the cup to hold the snail is a good idea!*

- Try not to intervene when he uses an item incorrectly unless it is unsafe. For example, if he tries to stand on a paper cup to become taller, he will quickly learn that the cup will not work that way.

Another idea

Spend a few days observing your own behavior. Notice tasks that you do for your child that he can begin to do for himself if the tools are handy. Allow him to use more tools such as tape, boxes, safe scissors, a small wheelbarrow, a small step stool, washable markers, or a bucket. Don't restrict him from using them in new ways unless his actions are unsafe.

Let's read together!

Tools
by Taro Miura

Painting on Paper

I see you using purple paint.

I'm painting.

Provide your child with paper, paintbrushes, and one or two colors of paint.

Your child's creativity will grow when you offer her a variety of painting experiences.

THE
CREATIVE CURRICULUM®
LearningGames®
Copyright 2007 Joseph Sparling

Why this is important

At this age, your child may naturally experiment with many original ways of doing things. With paint, she has many opportunities to express her original ideas without instruction. Early creative experiences can help to enrich the later, more cautious stages of your child's artistic development.

What you do

- Place painting materials on a low, flat table surface protected with newspapers, or put a few newspapers on the floor to use as a work space.

- Offer your child a paint smock. An old adult shirt worn backwards also works well.

- Allow your child plenty of time to explore with the paint and brushes.

- Stay nearby as your child paints, but wait until she finishes before offering comments: *You made a big red shape and some long blue lines. That's a wonderful painting!*

- Increase the number of paint colors after she feels comfortable with the painting process. You also can offer different colors of paper and different sizes of brushes or sponges to paint with.

Another idea

Find a space in your home to display your child's art. You can talk about her work and encourage her to describe it to others.

Let's read together!

The Dot
by Peter H. Reynolds

Matching Among Similar Pictures

Let your child look for one matching pair among several pictures of the same kind of thing, for example, among several pictures of cars.

Your child will begin to notice which pictures are nearly alike and which are exactly alike.

You found the match! Those other pictures didn't fool you.

Why this is important

Challenging your child to observe and make careful choices from among a group of similar items encourages her to pay attention to details. This skill will help your child as she learns to quickly and accurately see the differences between letters of the alphabet, including letters with similar shapes such as *b* and *d*.

What you do

- Cut out pictures of the same kinds of items in a catalog or magazine.

- Begin the game with four pictures on the table. The pictures should be similar, but with only two that are identical. For example, four pictures of coats, two of which are exactly the same.

- Invite your child to play with you as you ask: *Can you find the two coats that are the same?* When she succeeds, acknowledge her achievement: *You found the two red coats that match!*

- Ask your child to hide her eyes as you switch the positions of the pictures, remove the previously matching pair, and add a new matching pair to the group.

- Play the game with the first set of pictures several times before moving on to a new group of similar pictures.

Ready to move on?

Create a game that uses all the pictures. Spread every picture randomly on the table and invite your child to find each matching set.

Let's read together!

A Hen, A Chick and a String Guitar
by Margaret Read MacDonald

That's Mine!

That's my horse!

Encourage your child to protect her rights and express her needs with words.

With your help, your child can learn to use words rather than physical acts to satisfy her needs and rights.

Why this is important

Your child needs to learn to protect her rights and feelings with words rather than actions. Although she may occasionally use physical aggression because of her limited vocabulary, she eventually will stand up for herself instead of hitting. Your child can learn to express herself in appropriately assertive ways by simply and clearly saying what she needs or wants.

What you do

● Help your child practice using words instead of actions to express her needs. For example:

A personal choice	*I want a …(banana).*
An ordinary need	*I need my…(potty).*
An alternative to physical aggression	*That's my…(doll).*
A self-protective statement	*I don't like…(to be hit).*

● Observe your child carefully so that you can recognize the need for these expressive statements and specifically encourage her to use them: *Thank you for telling me that was your car. I'm sorry she took it away from you.* Or, *You used words to tell her you don't like to be hit. Now she knows how you feel.*

Another idea

Help your child anticipate the need for using clear statements by role-playing with her. You can create scenarios involving various emotions or physical needs.

Let's read together!

Hands Are Not for Hitting
by Martine Agassi, Ph.D.

I Look Great

You dressed yourself.

You look great!

Place a full-length mirror where your child can use it.

You can help your child know how he looks and feel good about his reflection in the mirror.

Why this is important

A full-length mirror helps your child know what his body looks like as a whole. He can begin to take more responsibility for grooming himself by using the mirror when combing his hair or getting dressed. He may enjoy simply staring at his reflection and smiling at the image. Studying the mirror reinforces his self-image as he learns to notice the color of his eyes and what his face looks like. A positive self-image builds confidence as he grows.

What you do

- Provide a full-length mirror for your child to use daily.

- Help him get dressed and encourage his efforts. *You put your shirt on by yourself. You look great! Do you want to look at yourself in the mirror?*

- Suggest dressing in front of the mirror on occasion so that he can see how his shirt looks as he buttons it or how his pants look as he pulls them on.

- Invite him to comb his hair in front of the mirror. Show him that you think he is capable by not fixing his hair after he combs it.

- Offer him privacy as he becomes comfortable dressing and grooming in front of the mirror.

Another idea

Your child might occasionally enjoy sharing the mirror with another child. The children can see their full images side by side and notice the similarities and differences.

Let's read together!

When I Feel Good About Myself
by Cornelia Maude Spelman

Packing My Own Picnic

You're spreading it well.

Invite your child to pack a special picnic lunch and decide what to include.

Packing a picnic allows your child to act independently and learn from his choices.

Why this is important

Your child probably likes to complete tasks on his own. In this activity he can work independently and his mistakes will have minimal consequences. An important thing for him to learn about independence is that sometimes things do not go as planned. Handling the problems of a poorly packed lunch is a gentle introduction to the risks of problems with later responsibilities, such as getting school supplies together in a backpack.

What you do

- Invite your child to join you on a picnic. Suggest that he first pack a lunch to take with him.

- Go with him to the kitchen and point out available items for packing.

- Talk about where he will be eating, such as in the backyard or at the park, and what foods might be convenient to eat there.

- Lay out the food items as you talk, along with several sandwich bags for him to use. Help him remember where to find his lunchbox or a paper bag.

- Stay in the kitchen while he works, but help only if asked. *I'll be here in the kitchen for a few minutes. Let me know if you need some help.*

- Remember that this is an exercise in independence but you can control his diet by limiting his food choices to healthy items only.

Another idea

When you repeat this game, it might help your child if you remind him of the outcome of the previous picnic: *Last time the pudding leaked out, remember?* He still may make a few poor choices, but you can remind him of what he learned from his prior experiences.

Let's read together!

Hungry Harry
by Joanne Partis

Wear the Turn Hat

It's Christopher's turn now.

Jon, please pass him the turn hat.

Invite your child and one or two friends to play a follow-the-leader game in which each person takes a turn wearing the hat and leading.

Using a hat to represent the current leader in the game can help your child learn to take turns.

THE
CREATIVE CURRICULUM®
LearningGames®
Copyright 2007 Joseph Sparling

Why this is important

Using a physical symbol, such as a hat, may help your child understand the idea of taking turns in a game. Your child may enjoy the importance of wearing the hat as he learns about cooperation. Using friendly language such as *passing the turn hat* instead of *giving up your turn* helps your child understand that his turn will come again soon.

What you do

- Find a special hat for the game.

- Invite your child and two friends to play: *Let's play Follow the Leader. This hat will tell us whose turn it is to be the leader.*

- Choose one child and say: *Jon, will you be the leader? You can put on the hat so we'll all know it's your turn.*

- Encourage the leader to perform an action, such as touching his nose. The other children will then copy his movements. Give each child a few minutes at a time with the hat.

Another idea

You can play this game one-on-one with your child at home to help him share leadership. In a group, you can use the hat to mark each child's turn to pass out spoons, pull the wagon, or lead a song.

Let's read together!

Share and Take Turns
by Cheri J. Meiners

Plan an Event

Here is our shopping list.

You found the cake mix.

Plan for a special event with your child by creating a shopping list, gathering all items needed, and reviewing the steps in the process.

Your child can learn to plan and feel included in the family.

Why this is important

Your child will find shopping with a purpose and a list more satisfying than simply accompanying an adult to the store. He can begin to understand the process of planning as he participates in a special event as an equal member. As your child's activities become more complex, he will need to think about materials needed and steps to be taken. Planning an event with you gives him practice in thinking ahead and following through.

What you do

- Include your child in planning for a special event, such as baking a cake for a relative's birthday: *Next week is Granddaddy's birthday. Do you think he might like a birthday cake?*

- Talk with your child about what is needed for the event, and make a list together. *Cake mix, icing, candles,* etc.

- Invite your child to participate in making a picture list of the needed items using magazines, scissors, paper, and glue. Help him find pictures of the needed items, cut them out, and glue them to the list.

- Take your child to the supermarket and offer minimal guidance as he chooses an item to find on the list.

- Review the shopping process at home with your child: *We were smart to plan. We have everything for Granddaddy's cake.*

Another idea

Simple planning can also be done for making a jack-o-lantern, setting up a child's birthday party, or preparing for a special cultural celebration.

Let's read together!

Bunny Party
by Rosemary Wells

Who, What, Where?

Who has on blue shoes?

Gary's shoes are blue!

Throughout your day, ask your child *who*, *what*, and *where* questions that will encourage him to describe people, objects, and places.

You encourage conversation with your child by posing questions that your child can answer.

Why this is important

Answering basic questions gives your child the chance to use many of the words he knows and encourages him to learn new words. By following your child's answer with more conversation about the topic, you help him describe people, objects, and places. Questions beginning with *who, what,* and *where* will guide him throughout his life in telling and interpreting stories.

What you do

- Include simple questions in your daily conversations with your child using the words *who, what* and *where. Who is coming to visit? What sound do you hear? Where's a good place to hide?*

- Use your child's answers as a starting point for further back-and-forth conversation on the same topic.

- Keep your questions short and casual. Your child may be reluctant to participate if you appear too insistent with your questions.

Let's read together!

Who Likes Rain?
by Wong Herbert Yee

Another idea

Use questions to encourage your child's creative thinking. Create an imaginary scenario and encourage your child to respond to your questions about it. *If we were going to have a big party for all of the animals at the zoo, whom would you invite? What would we do at the party?*

That Doesn't Belong

What doesn't belong on the table?

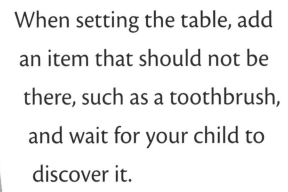

When setting the table, add an item that should not be there, such as a toothbrush, and wait for your child to discover it.

Your child will develop a clearer understanding of a group by noticing an object that does not belong in the group.

The toothbrush!

Why this is important

Pointing out an object that does not belong helps your child express the reasons why something belongs or does not belong. Noticing the item that is not part of the group helps her clarify her understanding of group membership.

What you do

- Finish setting the table by placing an odd object, such as a toothbrush or a book, near a plate.

- Say to your child: *Something doesn't look right. Would you please come and help me see what doesn't belong?*

- Show her the setting and tell her: *I was setting the table with things we use to eat. But something is there that shouldn't be. Can you see what it is?*

- Draw her attention to it, if necessary, by commenting on the appropriate items on the table: *I know we need a spoon, a cup, and a napkin.*

- Give positive feedback when she correctly locates the object. *You're right! That toothbrush shouldn't be there.*

Another idea

Increase the number of odd objects to be found. Think of other ways to incorporate the game into your time together: a pencil stuck into a crayon box, a sock in the washcloth drawer, etc.

Let's read together!

There's A Cow in the Cabbage Patch by Clare Beaton

Ball in the Bucket

Wow! You threw the ball into the bucket!

With your child, practice throwing a ball into a bucket. Increase the throwing distance as his skills improve.

Gradually, your child will gain more control in throwing.

THE
CREATIVE CURRICULUM®
LearningGames®
Copyright 2007 Joseph Sparling

Why this is important

By this age, children are well aware that throwing is usually done with a purpose, as in basketball or other sports. Throwing a ball at a large target helps your child learn to control and direct his own body movements. He must control his body in order to perform this or other specific actions.

What you do

- Provide a container such as a box, basket, tub, or bucket, a ball for your child, and a ball for yourself.

- Invite your child to stand with you a few feet away from the bucket.

- Throw your ball into the bucket as your child does the same. *Watch me throw the ball. Can you do it, too?*

- Move the bucket closer to him if he misses, and encourage him to try again.

- Describe his accuracy when appropriate: *You're getting it right where you want it!*

- Change the game by adding water to the bucket.

Ready to move on?

You can increase the difficulty by moving the bucket farther away or finding a container with a smaller opening.

Let's read together!

The Story of Red Rubber Ball
by Constance Kling Levy

An Errand for Two

Jack, you may take the note.

Les, you bring the books back in your basket.

Invite your child and a friend or sibling to share an errand in which both children have a specific duty to perform.

Your child may enjoy taking a responsible part in a cooperative activity.

THE
CREATIVE CURRICULUM®
Learning Games®

Why this is important

Sharing an errand teaches your child that cooperation means doing his expected part in an activity. Taking pleasure in needed activities done cooperatively is an important part of being a member of a group.

What you do

- Invite your child and a friend or sibling to go on an errand together. Whether inside or outside, keep safety in mind as you send them. The children do not need to be out of your sight for this game. Explain that you need them to do something to help you.

- Give each child a specific responsibility. Make sure they understand their roles before sending them out. For example, one child might take a note to a next-door neighbor asking for some flour. The other might carry back the flour.

- Review the result when they return: *You two did a great job together. Jack, it was important for you to get the note there. And Leslie, you did a good job carrying. Thanks for coming back so quickly.*

Another idea

Your child and his friend can go to the kitchen to bring back snacks or to an adjoining room for art supplies.

Let's read together!

Miki's First Errand
by Yoriko Tsutsui

Changing Partner Roles

You're handling the plates carefully.

Junior Partner

Partner with your child in an activity that allows her to move gradually from less to more responsibility.

Experimenting with partner roles helps your child learn to lead as well as follow.

Senior Partner

Where do you want me to put these?

THE
CREATIVE CURRICULUM®
LearningGames®
Copyright 2007 Joseph Sparling

Why this is important

Your child is old enough to experience responsibility in various helper, partner, and leadership roles. Different situations require differing balances of cooperation and leadership. Children need experience in these three roles if they are to function well in group situations.

What you do

- Use the simple task of setting the table to guide your child through various leadership roles.

- Invite your child to help you set the table. In this junior partner role she helps you as you lead the task. *Can you please place the forks and plates on the table?*

- Move to equal partnership for this task when she feels comfortable with helping you set the table. Together, decide who will put what on the table: *I'll be responsible for the serving dishes. What do you plan to put on the table?*

- Watch for signs that your child is ready to take full responsibility for setting the table. Assign her the leadership or senior partner role so that she knows she will place most of the items on the table and give you directions on where to place the rest.

Let's read together!

Jamaica Tag-Along
by Juanita Havill

Another idea

You can plan other activities that will allow your child to move through these three roles. For example, you could make paper mosaics. At first you direct the cutting and placement of the paper pieces. With the next mosaic, you could both share the responsibility. Finally, she could make all decisions about a third mosaic and give you directions.

Say What Just Happened

Yes, you copied what I did. Now can you tell me in words?

Watch what I'm going to do.

Ask your child to watch you perform an action such as touching your shoulders or hopping on one foot. Then encourage him to talk about what you just did.

Your child will learn to observe carefully and begin to use words to describe what he recently saw.

THE CREATIVE CURRICULUM®
LearningGames®

Copyright 2007 Joseph Sparling

Why this is important

You are giving your child a chance to use his growing vocabulary to report events accurately. His narrative skills will improve as he practices describing an action in detail. Describing what he sees helps him remember the event and enables him to communicate what he knows to others. It prepares your child to be able to follow and understand a sequence of events in written material.

What you do

- Draw your child's attention to something you're doing. Then, after you have stopped doing it, ask, *What did I do?*

- Notice how his first response may be to imitate the action. It may take a number of trials before he understands that you are asking for a clear description rather than action.

- Respond to any short answer he offers: *Yes, I did jump. Now watch again. Can you see more?*

- Repeat the action and the question: *What did I do?* He may add to the description: *You hopped on one foot.*

- Keep your responses positive so that your child stays motivated during the game.

- Try combining two actions and asking your child to describe them.

Another Idea

Help him get ready for paying attention in school by using classroom materials in the game. Make an X on a sheet of paper and then fold the paper in half. Ask your child to recall the action. Repeat the motion until he can fully describe what you did.

Let's read together!

Hondo and Fabian
by Peter McCarty

Changing Things

What happened to the water when we put it in the freezer?

Fill an ice cube tray with water, freeze it, and talk about the changes with your child.

You can encourage your child's curiosity in changes that occur around her every day.

THE
CREATIVE CURRICULUM®
LearningGames®
Copyright 2007 Joseph Sparling

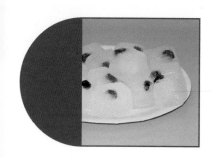

Why this is important

Freezing ice cubes with your child helps her become aware that objects can change and then return to their original state. Recognizing change is an important aspect of reasoning. Creating a change and then reversing it is one type of mathematical check.

What you do

- Begin by pointing out and naming *ice* and *water* to your child.

- Invite her to fill an empty ice cube tray with water. Ask her to add a raisin to each section of the tray. This will help her identify the water when it changes state.

- Put the tray in the freezer. Come back to the freezer after a nap, play, or errand.

- Remove the tray from the freezer and ask, *Where's our water? This doesn't look like water. What's this cold, cold stuff?*

- Talk with your child about the raisins frozen in the ice, using the words *change* and *same*.

- Add the ice cubes to a bowl of water, and encourage her to stir the water. Observe with her as the ice returns to water, and talk about the change.

- Limit your explanation of why the water changes. Your child will probably lose interest in a very scientific explanation.

Another idea

Try the game using a balloon. Ask your child what she thinks the balloon will look like after you blow it up. Other changeable objects that will work are open book/closed book, leaves scattered/leaves raked, and paper flat/ paper formed into a tube.

Let's read together!

Rain
by Manya Stojic

Remembering Pictures

1. Look at the single picture.
2. Put it away.
3. Find it on the big page.

You found the one you saw earlier.

Show your child a cutout picture, put it away, and then encourage him to find it again on a page of pictures.

Your child's memory will expand as he increases his ability to recall what he has seen.

THE
CREATIVE CURRICULUM®
LearningGames®

Why this is important

You can help with memory development by having your child look for a picture he has seen before. Systematic searching makes the task easier. The ability to recall visual memories of letter forms and symbols is especially important for reading, writing, and using computers.

What you do

- Find two identical copies of a catalog. Cut out pictures of a variety of items from one catalog such as a purse, lawn mower, and table.

- Mark the pages of the other catalog that feature the items you cut out.

- Sit on the floor with your child and give him one cutout to hold.

- Explain, *Here's something to take a good look at.*

- Put the picture out of sight when he gives it back to you.

- Open the uncut catalog to the page that contains the picture he just saw. Ask, *Can you point to the one you just saw?* If he cannot find it, close the catalog and show him the cutout again. Then return to the catalog.

- Congratulate him when he finds the picture, even if he needed help.

Ready to move on?

Make the game harder by showing him several cutouts at once, then put them all away, and have him find the pictures on different pages.

Let's read together!

There Was an Old Lady Who Swallowed a Fly
by Simms Taback

Copy Each Other

I can, you can, march.

March, march, march!

Play an imitation game with your child, saying your actions as you do them.

Your child will have an opportunity to say words that help her lead or follow.

Why this is important

Children like to try new ways to move, and they like to do what you do. You can make it fun to practice the following and leading skills that grow into cooperation. Knowing the names for her actions allows her to better explain what is happening. When she can describe what she is doing, she can take the leader's role in many games.

What you do

● Perform an action as you say or sing a verse.

> *I can, you can.*
> *Hop, hop, hop.*

● Use motions you have noticed your child learning, such as: hopping on one foot, skipping a step, jumping with both feet, etc.

● Use a single word to describe each action so that she can easily repeat the word. Try *nod, tap, clap, jump, bend,* or *march.* She will interpret the word by watching your actions.

● Change the game by inviting her to lead and choose the action.

Another idea

Encourage your child to play this game with a small group of friends. Everyone has a turn as the leader, and each child chooses the motion when she leads.

Let's read together!

Elizabeth's Doll
by Stephanie Stuve-Bodeen

Saying All I See

Two people are riding in that red car.

Yes!

Invite your child to describe what she sees in a detailed picture.

This game gives her practice using her growing vocabulary.

Why this is important

Reporting is one of the basic ways language is used. Although your child will likely identify people and objects first, eventually she will include actions and details.

Reporting visible information correctly is a step toward some of the more difficult forms of thinking such as reasoning or evaluating.

What you do

● Find an interesting page in a magazine or children's book. The page should have a detailed picture or several pictures so that your child will find plenty to talk about.

● Ask your child to describe what is on the page. Give her time to look and think before answering.

● Listen for names of objects, descriptions of actions, and words that tell about details such as size and shape.

● Encourage your child to explore the picture further by asking simple questions such as: *What size is the gorilla? How many apples are there? Is there something outside the window? What's the little boy doing? Could you tell me more about the things at the bottom of the page?*

Ready to move on?

Change the game by finding pictures with increasing amounts of detail. Your child should find and label more objects and actions as she develops her vocabulary and attention to detail.

Let's read together!

The Wide Mouthed Frog
by Keith Faulkner

Remembering Things and Places

Watch where we put each thing.

Show your child two or three toys placed around the room, and then reposition them as she closes her eyes so that she can guess what changed in the room.

Your child will learn to organize her memory as she practices linking places and objects.

Mousie's gone!

THE
CREATIVE CURRICULUM®
LearningGames®

Why this is important

We all need to remember where we put things so we can find them later. Memory is one of the tools we use in solving both simple and complex problems. Your child will learn to first link pairs of objects and places and then call them back from her memory.

What you do

- Put two or three familiar objects on the table and invite your child to name them.

- Ask her to look away, and then remove one of the objects. When she looks again, encourage her to tell you what is missing from the group.

- Move on to a more complex version of the game by asking her to help you find and name two common household objects, such as a ball and cup, or a toy truck and toy mouse.

- Put each item in a particular place, and say, *Let's put the truck right here on this table. Where shall we put the mouse? How about under the table!*

- Ask your child to review where each object is before closing her eyes or leaving the room while you change something.

- Remove one item and ask your child to return.

- Wait for her to discover what happened and tell it in her own way. She may say something like: *Mousie's not under the table anymore.* Give her positive feedback.

Ready to move on?

Slowly increase the difficulty of the game by adding one or two more items or by removing more than one item.

Let's read together!

Where Are You, Blue Kangaroo?
by Emma Chichester Clark

Props for Pretending

I'll cook something good to eat.

Chef

Doctor/Nurse

Stock a box with supplies that encourage your child to imagine herself in different roles.

Your child's thinking may expand as she dresses up to play various parts.

Why this is important

You can encourage your child to use pretending as a way of trying out situations she has not yet experienced. Pretending with props lets her practice future situations and make decisions as well as expand her creativity.

What you do

- Help your child collect and store the props she needs to play different roles. If possible, keep a separate box for each set of props.

- Store the boxes where she can get them out easily on her own.

- Try a few of these examples to get started:

A box with...	To be a...
Dolls, cloths, baby bottle	parent
Aprons, pans, spoons	cook
Book bag, notepad, keys	office worker
Tools, measuring tape, safety goggles	builder
Bandages, blanket, toy thermometer	doctor or nurse

- Limit the contents of each box so that your child is not overwhelmed.

- Add to or change the items in the box as you find more appropriate props.

- Help your child get started by asking: *Can you think of a person who would use these pans and spoons?*

Another idea

At cleanup time, ask your child to help put each item back in the appropriate box. She will need to think about what each object is used for in order to determine where it belongs.

Let's read together!

What Do People Do All Day?
by Richard Scarry

What Will Happen Next?

What will happen when I pour the syrup?

In the middle of a process, pause and ask your child, *What do you think will happen next?*

You will be giving your child a reason to purposely think ahead and to look for connections between events.

Chocolate milk.

You were right!

Why this is important

Thinking ahead about changes is a necessary step in scientific experimentation. Your child will learn to experiment with objects to determine if his predictions are correct. Predicting is an essential skill in adapting specific knowledge to your own needs. For example, a hammer that can drive nails can be predicted to also crack nutshells.

What you do

- Show your child a small empty box. Turn it over in your hand, and shake it for your child to see: *This is a quiet box. It doesn't make any noise when I shake it.* Hand it to your child to shake.

- Drop a marble into the box, and before shaking it say, *If I shake this box, what will happen next?*

- Wait for him to find words for what he believes will happen. After he makes his prediction, shake the box.

- Review the prediction with your child: *You thought it would make noise. And you were right!*

- Respond to an incorrect prediction after shaking the box by giving him a chance to make a second prediction.

- Describe what actually happened, rather than commenting negatively on the inaccurate predictions, if none of his predictions are accurate. *Putting something in the box makes it rattle when we shake it.*

Another idea

Think of other activities that your child can make predictions about: stirring chocolate into milk, sitting on a balloon, lowering an orange into a full cup of water, etc.

Let's read together!

If You Give a Pig a Pancake
by Laura Numeroff

Letters in My Name

Yes, and you traced it with your finger.

J.

Teach your child the letters in his name by first saying them, then pointing them out in print, and finally tracing the shape of each letter with him.

Your child will eventually remember the letters and begin to understand that letters make words.

THE CREATIVE CURRICULUM®
LearningGames®

Why this is important

The letters of your child's name provide a good beginning for learning letters. Your child will become aware of letters as symbols and recognize the sound and sight of the letters in his name. Learning to recognize the letters of his written name is part of early literacy.

What you do

- Make a point of saying and spelling your child's name together by saying: *Joey, J-O-E-Y. Can you come here, please?* He will begin to associate the letters with his name.

- Try getting his attention using only the letters once he becomes familiar with them. The next step will be helping him learn to recognize the letters.

- Point out one letter at a time until he can recognize all the letters of his name. Cereal boxes, magazines, signboards, toys, and labels provide good sources of big, colorful letters.

- Trace the letter with your finger when you see it and encourage your child to do the same.

- Use his knowledge of circles and lines when you're acquainting him with the letter: *An O is a circle. An E is four straight lines. A J is curved at the bottom.*

- Encourage him to remember any associations he makes, such as a *J* resembles a candy cane.

Another idea

Use consistent language when he learns to write his letters. The same descriptions will help him remember the shape of each letter in his name. If his interest continues, help him recognize additional letters beyond those in his name.

Let's read together!

Matthew A.B.C.
by Peter Catalanotto

How Did You Feel When ...?

> How did you feel when you climbed to the top?

After a game of physical activity, share a quiet moment with your child as you both think back on and talk about your feelings during the game.

Recalling feelings right after they have happened will help your child learn how to explain himself to others.

THE
CREATIVE CURRICULUM®
LearningGames®
Copyright 2007 Joseph Sparling

Why this is important

You can ask questions in a way that will help your child recall and tell about how he was feeling during an active play experience. When he hears the question immediately after the experience, he can put together the recent actions with the feelings he had at that time. Understanding his feelings helps him to make decisions about trying an activity again. The remembrance of a sensory feeling helps to recall the word for it.

What you do

- Sit quietly with your child after an active session of exciting play such as riding a bike or playing ball. Ask, *Can you tell me what was the hardest thing you just did?*

- Wait as your child recalls the experience. Respond to his answer by repeating it back to him and adding a question: *Pushing your feet was hard. But you did it anyway, didn't you?*

- Suggest a few choices if he cannot remember: *Was it steering? Was it catching the ball in time?*

- Ask him other questions to help him remember the feel of the experience: *What felt the easiest? The scariest? The best?* Give him choices and ideas if needed.

Another idea

As he becomes comfortable with this activity, wait longer before asking him to recall. Do you remember how it felt when the ball was coming to you?

Let's read together!

Feelings: A First Poem Book About Feelings
by Felicia Law